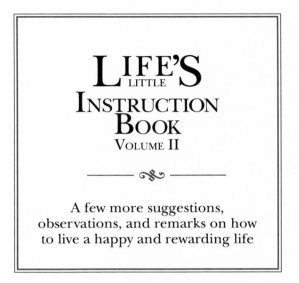

LIFE'S LITTLE INSTRUCTION BOOK
VOLUME II

A few more suggestions,
observations, and remarks on how
to live a happy and rewarding life

H. JACKSON BROWN, Jr.

Rutledge Hill Press
Nashville, Tennessee

Published in Nashville, Tennessee, by Rutledge Hill Press, Inc.,
211 Seventh Avenue North, Nashville, Tennessee 37219.
Distributed in Canada by H. B. Fenn and Company Ltd.,
Mississauga, Ontario.

Typography by D&T/Bailey Typesetting, Nashville, Tennessee

Library of Congress Cataloging-in-Publication Data

Brown, H. Jackson, 1940–
    Life's little instruction book by H. Jackson Brown, Jr.
    p.   cm.
    ISBN 1-55853-275-7
    1. Happiness—Quotations, maxims, etc.   2. Conduct of life—
    Quotations, maxims, etc.   I. Title.
    BJ1481.B87   1991   91-9800
170:44—dc20   CIP

Printed in the United States of America
2 3 4 5 6 7 8 9—97 96 95 94

Introduction

❧

LIFE is a process. We are all works in progress—green tomatoes ripening on the windowsill of life. As I experience more, learn more, and contemplate more, I often think of what use my discoveries might be to my son, Adam.

Several years ago I jotted down a list of advice for him as he left home to begin college. At the time I thought the list was fairly complete. But within a few days of presenting him with the 32 typed pages that became *Life's Little Instruction Book,* I began to think of other entries I wished I had included. How could I have forgotten to mention "Never be the first to break a family tradition," or "Believe in love at first sight," or practical advice like "Overpay good baby sitters" and "Never drive while holding a cup of hot coffee between your knees"? Obviously there was only one thing to do—start another list. I promised myself I wouldn't send it to him until it reached at least 512 entries—one more than the original list. It took two years to complete.

The day Adam received it, he called from his apartment. "Dad," he said, "this new list is terrific. I think it's more useful than the first one. Does this mean I should look for a new volume of *Life's Little Instruction Book* every two years?" "Would you like that?" I asked. "Oh, yes," he said. "I'll see what I can do," I replied, with not a small degree of satisfaction.

Little does Adam know that I can no more stop writing down these suggestions and observations than I could stop at a doughnut shop and order only coffee.

Life keeps coming at me, and new insights and discoveries get caught in my net. Like a fisherman, I haul them up, sort the catch, and head for the harbor. It's late and getting dark. But up ahead, standing on the dock, is a young man holding a lantern welcoming me. It's my son, Adam.

Other books by H. Jackson Brown, Jr.

A Father's Book of Wisdom
P.S., I Love You
Life's Little Instruction Book
Live and Learn and Pass It On
Wit and Wisdom from the Peanut Butter Gang

· 512 ·

Believe in love at first sight.

· 513 ·

Never laugh at anyone's dreams.

· 514 ·

Overpay good baby sitters.

· 515 ·

Never refuse jury duty.
It is your civic responsibility, and you'll learn a lot.

· 516 ·

Accept a breath mint if someone offers you one.

· 517 ·

When you feel terrific, notify your face.

· 518 ·

Love deeply and passionately.
You might get hurt, but it's the only way
to live life completely.

· 519 ·

Never apologize for being early
for an appointment.

· 520 ·

Open the car door for your wife
and always help her with her coat.

· 521 ·

Discipline with a gentle hand.

· 522 ·

When reconvening after a conference break,
choose a chair in a different
part of the room.

· 523 ·

Read the ten books nominated each
year for the ABBY Award.

· 524 ·

Rake a big pile of leaves every
fall and jump in it with someone you love.

· 525 ·

Volunteer. Sometimes the jobs no one
wants conceal big opportunities.

· 526 ·

Never drive while holding a cup
of hot coffee between your knees.

· 527 ·

Carry Handi-Wipes in your
glove compartment.

· 528 ·

Use a travel agent. It costs no more
and saves time and effort.

· 529 ·

Have a professional photo of yourself made.
Update it every three years.

· 530 ·

Never miss an opportunity to ride
a roller coaster.

· 531 ·

Never miss an opportunity to have
someone rub your back.

· 532 ·

Never miss an opportunity to sleep
on a screened-in porch.

· 533 ·

Sign all warranty cards
and mail them in promptly.

· 534 ·

Remember the advice of our friend Ken Beck:
When you see a box turtle
crossing the road, stop and put it
safely on the other side.

· 535 ·

Create a little signal only your wife knows
so that you can show her you
love her across a crowded room.

· 536 ·

Never be the first to break a
family tradition.

· 537 ·

Park next to the end curb in parking lots.
Your car doors will have half the
chance of getting dented.

· 538 ·

Keep a diary of your accomplishments
at work. Then when you ask for a raise,
you'll have the information you need
to back it up.

· 539 ·

Never sign contracts with blank spaces.

· 540 ·

Drive as you wish your kids would.
Never speed or drive recklessly
with children in the car.

· 541 ·

In disagreements, fight fairly.
No name calling.

· 542 ·

Never take the last piece of
fried chicken.

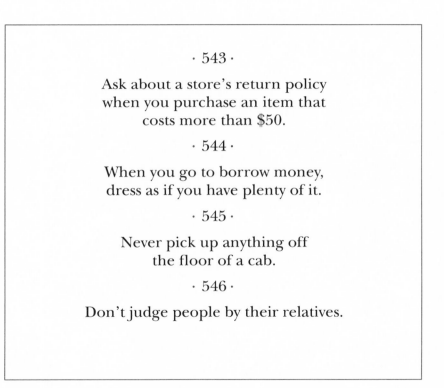

· 543 ·

Ask about a store's return policy
when you purchase an item that
costs more than $50.

· 544 ·

When you go to borrow money,
dress as if you have plenty of it.

· 545 ·

Never pick up anything off
the floor of a cab.

· 546 ·

Don't judge people by their relatives.

· 547 ·

Eat a piece of chocolate to cure bad breath
from onions or garlic.

· 548 ·

Seize every opportunity for additional
training in your job.

· 549 ·

When traveling,
leave the good jewelry at home.

· 550 ·

Put your address inside your luggage
as well as on the outside.

· 551 ·

Never give your credit card number
over the phone if you didn't
place the call.

· 552 ·

Remember that everyone you meet
is afraid of something, loves something,
and has lost something.

· 553 ·

Check hotel bills carefully,
especially the charges for local and
long-distance calls.

· 554 ·

Talk slow
but think quick.

· 555 ·

When someone asks you a question
you don't want to answer, smile and ask,
"Why do you want to know?"

· 556 ·

Don't admire people for their wealth
but for the creative and generous
ways they put it to use.

· 557 ·

Take along two big safety pins when you
travel so that you can pin the drapes shut
in your motel room.

· 558 ·

Never betray a confidence.

· 559 ·

Never claim a victory prematurely.

· 560 ·

Never leave the kitchen when
something's boiling on the stove.

· 561 ·

Say "bless you" when you hear
someone sneeze.

· 562 ·

Make the punishment fit the crime.

· 563 ·

Remember that just the moment you say,
"I give up," someone else seeing the same
situation is saying, "My, what a
great opportunity."

· 564 ·

Tour the main branch of the public library
on Fifth Avenue the next time you are in
New York City. Unforgettable.

· 565 ·

Never give anybody a fondue set or
anything painted avocado green.

· 566 ·

Don't let your family get so busy that you
don't sit down to at least one meal
a day together.

· 567 ·

Remember the three Rs:
Respect for self; Respect for others;
Responsibility for all your actions.

· 568 ·

Carry your own alarm clock when
traveling. Hotel wake-up calls are
sometimes unreliable.

· 569 ·

When you lose, don't lose the lesson.

· 570 ·

Keep the porch light on until all the family
is in for the night.

· 571 ·

Plant zucchini only if you have
lots of friends.

· 572 ·

Take along a small gift for the host or hostess
when you're a dinner guest.
A book is a good choice.

· 573 ·

Don't overlook life's small joys while
searching for the big ones.

· 574 ·

Keep a well-stocked first-aid kit in your
car and at home.

· 575 ·

Never be photographed with a
cocktail glass in your hand.

· 576 ·

Don't let a little dispute injure
a great friendship.

· 577 ·

Don't marry a woman who
picks at her food.

· 578 ·

Order a seed catalog. Read it on the
day of the first snowfall.

· 579 ·

Pack a compass and the Nature Company's
pocket survival tool when hiking in
unfamiliar territory.

· 580 ·

Read a book about beekeeping.

· 581 ·

When lost or in distress, signal in
"threes"—three shouts, three gunshots, or
three horn blasts.

· 582 ·

Don't be surprised to discover that luck
favors those who are prepared.

· 583 ·

When asked to play the piano, do it without
complaining or making excuses.

· 584 ·

Subscribe to *Consumer Reports* magazine.

· 585 ·

Don't expect your love alone to make a
neat person out of a messy one.

· 586 ·

Take off the convention badge as soon as
you leave the convention hall.

· 587 ·

Look for ways to make your
boss look good.

· 588 ·

Every so often, invite the person in line
behind you to go ahead of you.

· 589 ·

Carry a small pocket knife.

· 590 ·

Remember that the person who steals
an egg will steal a chicken.

· 591 ·

Meet regularly with someone who holds
vastly different views than you.

· 592 ·

Don't go looking for trouble.

· 593 ·

Don't buy someone else's trouble.

· 594 ·

Give people more than they expect and do it cheerfully.

· 595 ·

Be the first to fight for a just cause.

· 596 ·

When you have the choice of two
exciting things, choose the one
you haven't tried.

· 597 ·

Remember that no time spent with your
children is ever wasted.

· 598 ·

Remember that no time is ever wasted that
makes two people better friends.

· 599 ·

Avoid approaching horses and restaurants
from the rear.

· 600 ·

There are people who will always come up with
reasons why you can't do what you want to do.
Ignore them.

· 601 ·

Check to see if your regular car
insurance covers you when you rent a car.
The insurance offered by car rental
companies is expensive.

· 602 ·

If you need to bring in a business partner,
make sure your partner brings
along some money.

· 603 ·

Never say anything uncomplimentary
about another person's dog.

· 604 ·

If you have trouble with a company's products
or services, go to the top. Write
the president, then follow up
with a phone call.

· 605 ·

Don't ride in a car if the driver
has been drinking.

· 606 ·

Call the Better Business Bureau if you're not
sure about a business' reputation.

· 607 ·

Think twice before accepting
the lowest bid.

· 608 ·

Never miss a chance to dance
with your wife.

· 609 ·

When in doubt about what art to put
on a wall, choose a framed black-and-white
photo by Ansel Adams.

· 610 ·

When uncertain what to wear, a blue blazer,
worn with gray wool slacks, a white shirt,
and a red-and-blue striped silk tie,
is almost always appropriate.

· 611 ·

When boarding a bus, say "hello" to the driver.
Say "thank you" when you get off.

· 612 ·

Write a short note inside the front cover
when giving a book as a gift.

· 613 ·

Never give a gift that's not
beautifully wrapped.

· 614 ·

Make the rules for your children clear,
fair, and consistent.

· 615 ·

Don't think expensive equipment will make up
for lack of talent or practice.

· 616 ·

Learn to say "I love you" in French,
Italian, and Swedish.

· 617 ·

On a clear night, look for Orion's Belt
and think of your mother. It's her
favorite constellation.

· 618 ·

Memorize your favorite love poem.

· 619 ·

Ask anyone giving you directions
to repeat them at least twice.

· 620 ·

When you are totally exhausted but have
to keep going, wash your face and hands and
put on clean socks and a clean shirt.
You will feel remarkably refreshed.

· 621 ·

Make allowances for your friends'
imperfections as readily as you
do for your own.

· 622 ·

Steer clear of any place with a "Ladies Welcome"
sign in the window.

· 623 ·

When you realize you've made a mistake,
take immediate steps to correct it.

· 624 ·

Be ruthlessly realistic when it
comes to your finances.

· 625 ·

Smile when picking up the phone. The caller
will hear it in your voice.

· 626 ·

Set high goals for your employees and
help them attain them.

· 627 ·

Pay your bills on time. If you can't, write your
creditors a letter describing your situation.
Send them something every month,
even if it's only five dollars.

· 628 ·

Do your homework and know your facts, but
remember it's passion that persuades.

· 629 ·

Don't waste time trying to appreciate
music you dislike. Spend the time with
music you love.

· 630 ·

Always put something in the collection plate.

· 631 ·

When concluding a business deal
and the other person suggests
working out the details later,
say, "I understand, but I would like
to settle the entire matter right now."
Don't move from the table
until you do.

· 632 ·

Ask yourself if you would feel comfortable
giving your two best friends a key to
your house. If not, look for some
new best friends.

· 633 ·

Do the right thing,
regardless of what others think.

· 634 ·

Wear a shirt and tie to job interviews,
even for a job unloading boxcars.

· 635 ·

Judge people from where they stand,
not from where you stand.

· 636 ·

When shaking a woman's hand, squeeze it
no harder than she squeezes yours.

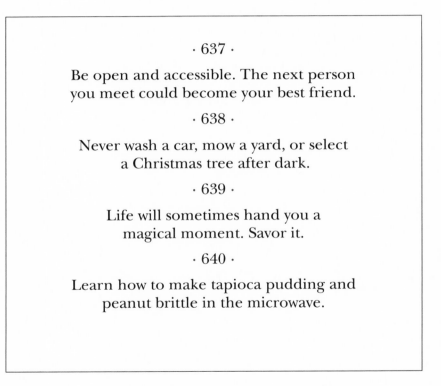

· 637 ·

Be open and accessible. The next person
you meet could become your best friend.

· 638 ·

Never wash a car, mow a yard, or select
a Christmas tree after dark.

· 639 ·

Life will sometimes hand you a
magical moment. Savor it.

· 640 ·

Learn how to make tapioca pudding and
peanut brittle in the microwave.

· 641 ·

Set aside your dreams for your children and
help them attain their own dreams.

· 642 ·

Dress a little better than your clients
but not as well as your boss.

643 ·

Take the stairs when it's four
flights or less.

· 644 ·

Never threaten if you don't intend
to back it up.

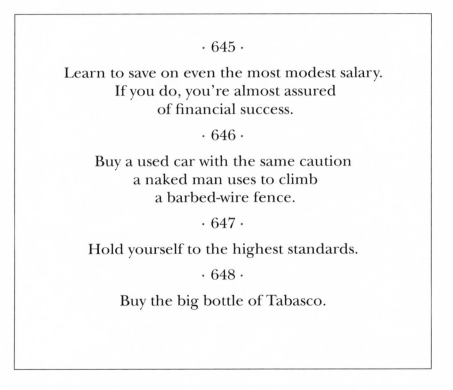

· 645 ·

Learn to save on even the most modest salary.
If you do, you're almost assured
of financial success.

· 646 ·

Buy a used car with the same caution
a naked man uses to climb
a barbed-wire fence.

· 647 ·

Hold yourself to the highest standards.

· 648 ·

Buy the big bottle of Tabasco.

· 649 ·

Don't confuse comfort with happiness.

· 650 ·

Don't confuse wealth with success.

· 651 ·

Be the first to forgive.

· 652 ·

When talking to your doctor,
don't let him or her interrupt or end the
session early. It's your body and your money.
Stay until all your questions are
answered to your satisfaction.

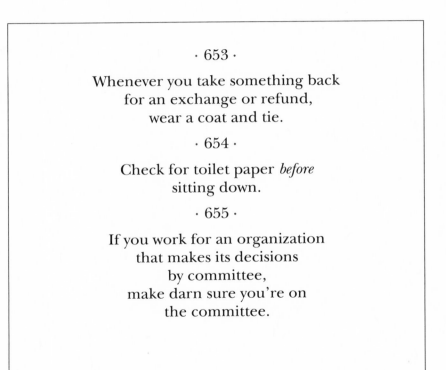

· 653 ·

Whenever you take something back
for an exchange or refund,
wear a coat and tie.

· 654 ·

Check for toilet paper *before*
sitting down.

· 655 ·

If you work for an organization
that makes its decisions
by committee,
make darn sure you're on
the committee.

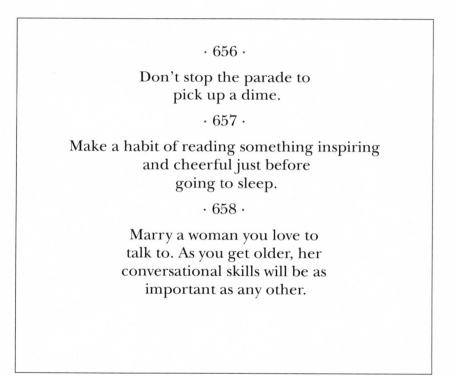

· 656 ·

Don't stop the parade to
pick up a dime.

· 657 ·

Make a habit of reading something inspiring
and cheerful just before
going to sleep.

· 658 ·

Marry a woman you love to
talk to. As you get older, her
conversational skills will be as
important as any other.

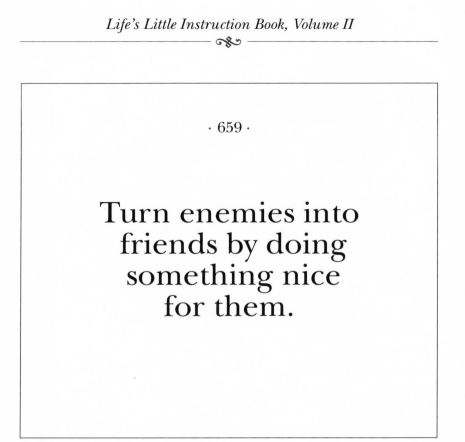

· 659 ·

Turn enemies into
friends by doing
something nice
for them.

· 660 ·

When hiring, give special consideration to
a man who is an Eagle Scout and a woman who
has received the Girl Scout Gold Award

· 661 ·

Be as friendly to the janitor as you are to the
chairman of the board.

· 662 ·

Mind your own business.

· 663 ·

Remember that a person who is foolish with
money is foolish in other ways too.

· 664 ·

If you want to do something and you feel
in your bones that it's the right thing
to do, do it. Intuition is often
as important as the facts.

· 665 ·

Don't cut corners.

· 666 ·

Learn to bake bread.

· 667 ·

Everyone loves praise. Look hard for ways
to give it to them.

· 668 ·

Spend some time alone.

· 669 ·

Be an original. If that means
being a little eccentric, so be it.

· 670 ·

Everybody deserves a birthday cake.
Never celebrate a birthday without one.

· 671 ·

Pay as much attention to the things that are
working positively in your life as you do
to those that are giving you trouble.

· 672 ·

Open your arms to change,
but don't let go of your values.

· 673 ·

When it comes to worrying or painting a picture,
know when to stop.

· 674 ·

Don't expect anyone to know what you want for
Christmas if you don't tell them.

· 675 ·

Before taking a long trip, fill your tank
and empty your bladder.

· 676 ·

Ask for double prints when you have film
processed. Send the extras to the
people in the photos.

· 677 ·

When taking a woman home, make sure
she's safely inside her house
before you leave.

· 678 ·

Live with your new pet several days before
you name it. The right name
will come to you.

· 679 ·

Every year celebrate the day you and
your wife had your first date.

· 680 ·

Treat your employees with the same respect
you give your clients.

· 681 ·

Slow down. I mean *really* slow down
in school zones.

· 682 ·

Allow your children to face the
consequences of their actions.

· 683 ·

Be quick to take advantage of an advantage.

· 684 ·

Don't expect the best gifts to come
wrapped in pretty paper.

· 685 ·

You may be fortunate and make a lot of money.
But be sure your work involves something
that enriches your spirit as well
as your bank account.

· 686 ·

When a good man or woman runs for
political office, support him or her
with your time and money.

· 687 ·

When you need professional advice, get it from
professionals, not from your friends.

· 688 ·

Remember that silence is sometimes
the best answer.

· 689 ·

Don't buy a cheap mattress.

· 690 ·

Don't think you can relax your way
to happiness. Happiness comes
as a result of *doing*.

· 691 ·

Don't dismiss a good idea simply because
you don't like the source.

· 692 ·

Pay for a poor child to go to summer camp.

· 693 ·

Choose a church that sings joyful music.

· 694 ·

What you must do, do cheerfully.

· 695 ·

Don't waste time waiting for inspiration.
Begin, and inspiration will find you.

· 696 ·

Don't believe all you
hear, spend all you
have, or sleep all
you want.

· 697 ·

When you say, "I love you," mean it.

· 698 ·

When you say, "I'm sorry," look
the person in the eye.

· 699 ·

Conduct yourself in such a way that your
high school would want you to address
the graduating seniors.

· 700 ·

Be engaged at least six months
before you get married.

· 701 ·

Win without boasting.

· 702 ·

Lose without excuses.

· 703 ·

Watch your attitude. It's the first thing
people notice about you.

· 704 ·

Pack a light bathrobe on overnight trips.
Take your pillow, too.

· 705 ·

Choose the apartment on the top floor.

· 706 ·

Ask someone you'd like to know better to list
five people he would most like to meet.
It will tell you a lot about him.

· 707 ·

Don't be a person who says,
"Ready, fire, aim."

· 708 ·

Don't be a person who says,
"Ready, aim, aim, aim."

· 709 ·

Deadlines are important. Meet them.

· 710 ·

When you find someone doing
small things well, put him or her
in charge of bigger things.

· 711 ·

Read more books.

· 712 ·

Watch less TV.

· 713 ·

Remember that a good price is not necessarily
what an object is marked, but
what it is worth to you.

· 714 ·

When opportunity
knocks, invite it
to stay for dinner.

· 715 ·

Remember that the more you know,
the less you fear.

· 716 ·

When a waitress or waiter provides
exceptional service, leave a generous tip,
plus a short note like, "Thanks
for the wonderful service. You made
our meal a special experience."

· 717 ·

Remove your sunglasses when
you talk to someone.

· 718 ·

Buy three best-selling children's books.
Read them and then give
them to a youngster.

· 719 ·

Introduce yourself to your neighbors
as soon as you move into
a new neighborhood.

· 720 ·

When a friend or loved one becomes ill,
remember that hope and positive
thinking are strong medicines.

· 721 ·

When you find something you really want,
don't let a few dollars keep
you from getting it.

· 722 ·

Be your children's best teacher
and coach.

· 723 ·

Some things need doing better than they've
ever been done before. Some just need
doing. Others don't need doing at all.
Know which is which.

· 724 ·

Buy ladders, extension cords, and garden hoses
longer than you think you'll need.

· 725 ·

Don't confuse mere inconveniences
with real problems.

· 726 ·

When asked to pray in public,
be quick about it.

· 727 ·

Show extra respect for people whose jobs
put dirt under their fingernails.

· 728 ·

Remember that
a good example
is the best sermon.

· 729 ·

Hold your child's hand every chance you get.
The time will come all too soon when
he or she won't let you.

· 730 ·

When you carve the Thanksgiving turkey,
give the first piece to the person
who prepared it.

· 731 ·

Live a good, honorable life. Then when you
get older and think back, you'll get
to enjoy it a second time.

· 732 ·

Wipe off the sticky honey jar before
putting it back on the shelf.

· 733 ·

Purchase one piece of original art each year,
even if it's just a small painting
by a high school student.

· 734 ·

Volunteer to help work a few hours each month
in a soup kitchen.

· 735 ·

Learn to juggle.

· 736 ·

Don't think people at the top of their
professions have all the answers.
They don't.

· 737 ·

Learn to make great spaghetti sauce.
Your mother's recipe is the best.

· 738 ·

If you're treated unfairly by an airline,
contact the Consumer Affairs Office of
the Department of Transportation
at (202) 366-2220.

· 739 ·

Get a car with a sun roof.

· 740 ·

Don't carry expensive luggage.
It's a tip-off to thieves that
expensive items may be inside.

· 741 ·

When traveling by plane, don't pack valuables
or important papers in your suitcase.
Carry them on board with you.

· 742 ·

Keep your private thoughts private.

· 743 ·

Put your jacket around your girlfriend
on a chilly evening.

· 744 ·

Once every couple of months enjoy a
four-course meal—but eat each course
at a different restaurant.

· 745 ·

Introduce yourself to someone you would like
to meet by smiling and saying, "My name is
Adam Brown. I haven't had the
pleasure of meeting you."

· 746 ·

Be humble and polite, but don't let
anyone push you around.

· 747 ·

Put the strap around your neck before
looking through binoculars.

· 748 ·

Do 100 push-ups every day: 50 in the
morning and 50 in the evening.

· 749 ·

Wear goggles when operating a
Weed Eater or power saw.

· 750 ·

Wrap a couple of thick rubber bands around
your wallet when you're fishing or hiking.
This will prevent it from slipping
out of your pocket.

· 751 ·

Don't expect bankers to come to
your aid in a crunch.

· 752 ·

Be advised that when negotiating,
if you don't get it in writing,
you probably won't get it.

· 753 ·

Don't do business with anyone who
has a history of suing people.

· 754 ·

Every so often let your spirit of adventure
triumph over your good sense.

· 755 ·

Use a favorite picture of a loved one
as a bookmark.

· 756 ·

Never lose your nerve, your
temper, or your car keys.

· 757 ·

Trust in God, but lock your car.

· 758 ·

Surprise an old friend with a phone call.

· 759 ·

Get involved at your child's school.

· 760 ·

Champion your wife. Be her best
friend and biggest fan.

· 761 ·

Add to your children's private library by
giving them a hardback copy of one
of the classics every birthday.
Begin with their first birthday.

· 762 ·

Carry a list of your wife's
important sizes in your wallet.

· 763 ·

Don't open credit card bills
on the weekend.

· 764 ·

Mind the store. No one cares about
your business the way you do.

· 765 ·

Don't say no until you've
heard the whole story.

· 766 ·

When you are a dinner guest, take a
second helping if it's offered,
but never a third.

· 767 ·

Never say anything uncomplimentary about
your wife or children in the
presence of others.

· 768 ·

Before going to bed on Christmas Eve,
join hands with your family and
sing "Silent Night."

· 769 ·

Don't accept unacceptable behavior.

· 770 ·

Never put the car in "drive" until all
passengers have buckled up.

· 771 ·

When eating at a restaurant that features
foreign food, don't order anything
you can fix at home.

· 772 ·

Send your mother-in-law flowers
on your wife's birthday.

· 773 ·

Write your pastor a note and tell him
how much he means to you.

· 774 ·

Write your favorite author
a note of appreciation.

· 775 ·

Apologize immediately when you lose your
temper, especially to children.

· 776 ·

Buy your fiancée the nicest
diamond engagement ring you can afford.

· 777 ·

When giving a speech, concentrate on what
you can give the audience, not what
you can get from them.

· 778 ·

Don't be so concerned with your rights
that you forget your manners.

· 779 ·

When you're uncertain of what you should
pay someone, ask, "What do you think
is fair?" You'll almost always get
a reasonable answer.

· 780 ·

Don't let weeds grow around your dreams.

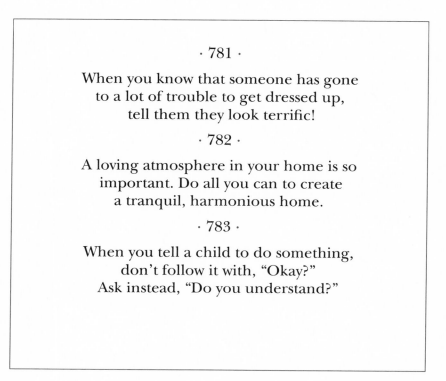

· 781 ·

When you know that someone has gone
to a lot of trouble to get dressed up,
tell them they look terrific!

· 782 ·

A loving atmosphere in your home is so
important. Do all you can to create
a tranquil, harmonious home.

· 783 ·

When you tell a child to do something,
don't follow it with, "Okay?"
Ask instead, "Do you understand?"

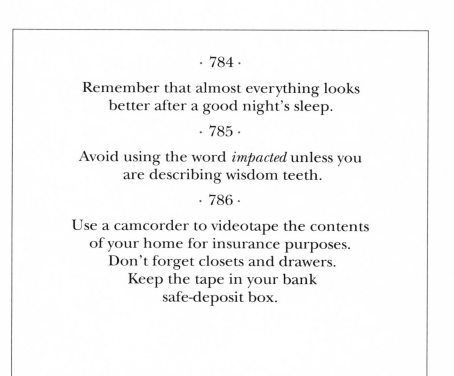

· 784 ·

Remember that almost everything looks
better after a good night's sleep.

· 785 ·

Avoid using the word *impacted* unless you
are describing wisdom teeth.

· 786 ·

Use a camcorder to videotape the contents
of your home for insurance purposes.
Don't forget closets and drawers.
Keep the tape in your bank
safe-deposit box.

· 787 ·

Read William Safire's *Lend Me Your Ears,*
a collection of the world's great speeches,
(W. W. Norton & Co., 1992).

· 788 ·

Keep a separate shaving kit packed
just for traveling.

· 789 ·

Remember that *how* you say something
is as important as *what* you say.

· 790 ·

Every so often watch "Sesame Street."

· 791 ·

Read between the lines.

· 792 ·

Get to garage sales early. The good stuff
is usually gone by 8:00 A.M.

· 793 ·

Stop and watch stonemasons at work.

· 794 ·

Stop and watch a farmer plowing a field.

· 795 ·

If your town has a baseball team,
attend the season opener.

· 796 ·

When you see visitors taking pictures of
each other, offer to take a picture
of their group together.

· 797 ·

In disagreements with loved ones,
deal with the current situation.
Don't bring up the past.

· 798 ·

Never apologize for extreme measures when
defending your values, your health,
or your family's safety.

· 799 ·

Don't think you can fill an emptiness
in your heart with money.

· 800 ·

Become famous for finishing
important, difficult tasks.

· 801 ·

Never sell your teddy bear, letter sweater, or
high school yearbooks at a garage sale.
You'll regret it later.

· 802 ·

Leave a quarter where a child can find it.

· 803 ·

Don't take good
friends, good health,
or a good marriage
for granted.

· 804 ·

Place a note reading "Your license number
has been reported to the police" on the
windshield of a car illegally parked
in a handicapped space.

· 805 ·

Buy a new tie to wear to your wedding
rehearsal dinner. Wear it only once.
Keep it forever.

· 806 ·

When you're lost, admit it,
and ask for directions.

· 807 ·

Never buy just one roll of toilet paper,
one roll of film, or one jar of peanut butter.
Get two.

· 808 ·

Do a good job because you want to,
not because you have to. This puts you
in charge instead of your boss.

· 809 ·

Remember that the shortest way to get
anywhere is to have good company
traveling with you.

· 810 ·

Never type a love letter.
Use a fountain pen.

· 811 ·

Never buy a chair or sofa without first
sitting on it for several minutes.

· 812 ·

Don't be thin-skinned. Take criticism as well
as praise with equal grace.

· 813 ·

At the end of your days, be leaning
forward—not falling backwards.

· 814 ·

Never eat liver at a restaurant.
Some things should be done only
in the privacy of one's home.

· 815 ·

Keep impeccable tax records.

· 816 ·

Clean out a different drawer in
your house every week.

· 817 ·

Share your knowledge.
It's a way to achieve immortality.

· 818 ·

Be gentle
with the Earth.

· 819 ·

Don't work for a company led by someone
of questionable character.

· 820 ·

When working with contractors,
include a penalty clause in your contract
for their not finishing on time.

· 821 ·

Read bulletin boards at the grocery store,
college bookstore, and coin laundry.
You will find all sorts of interesting
things there.

· 822 ·

The next time you're standing next to
a police officer, firefighter, or paramedic,
tell them that you appreciate what
they do for the community.

· 823 ·

Learn three knock-knock jokes
so that you will always be ready
to entertain children.

· 824 ·

Spend your time and energy creating,
not criticizing.

· 825 ·

Visit your old high school and introduce
yourself to the principal. Ask if you
can sit in on a couple of classes.

· 826 ·

Respect sailboats, snowmobiles, and
motorcycles. They can teach you
a painful lesson very fast.

· 827 ·

Act with courtesy and fairness regardless
of how others treat you. Don't let them
determine your response.

· 828 ·

In a verbal confrontation, lower your
voice to the degree that the other
person raises his or hers.

· 829 ·

Let your children see you do things for your
wife that lets them know how much
you love and treasure her.

· 830 ·

Take photographs of every car you own.
Later, these photos will trigger
wonderful memories.

· 831 ·

Don't allow children to ride in the
back of a pickup truck.

· 832 ·

When you are a dinner guest at a restaurant,
don't order anything more expensive
than your host does.

· 833 ·

When someone offers to pay you
now or later, choose now.

· 834 ·

Don't leave hair in the shower drain.

· 835 ·

When traveling the backroads,
stop whenever you see a sign that reads
"Honey For Sale."

· 836 ·

Start every day with the most important
thing you have to do. Save the less
important tasks for later.

· 837 ·

Think twice before deciding not to
charge for your work. People often don't
value what they don't pay for.

· 838 ·

Don't outlive your money.

· 839 ·

Never grab at a falling knife.

· 840 ·

Never take what you cannot use.

· 841 ·

When there is a hill to climb, don't think
that waiting will make it smaller.

· 842 ·

When your dog dies, frame his collar and
put it above a window facing west.

· 843 ·

When a garment label warns
"Dry Clean Only," believe it.

· 844 ·

Don't eat any meat loaf but your mom's.

· 845 ·

Write the date and the names
of non-family members on the backs
of all photos as soon as you get them
from the developer.

· 846 ·

Help a child plant a small garden.

· 847 ·

Pray.
There is
immeasurable
power in it.

· 848 ·

Don't take 11 items to the 10 Items
Express Check-Out lane.

· 849 ·

Don't call a fishing rod a "pole," a line a "rope,"
a rifle a "gun," or a ship a "boat."

· 850 ·

At meetings, resist turning around
to see who has just arrived late.

· 851 ·

Don't ride a bicycle or motorcycle
barefooted.

· 852 ·

Just because you earn a decent wage,
don't look down on those who don't.
To put things in perspective, consider what
would happen to the public good if you didn't
do your job for 30 days. Then, consider
the consequences if sanitation workers
didn't do their jobs for 30 days.
Now, whose job is more important?

· 853 ·

Don't purchase anything in a package that
appears to have been opened.

· 854 ·

Refuse to share personal and financial
information unless you feel
it is absolutely essential.

· 855 ·

Never do business with people who knock
on your door and say, "I just happened
to be in the neighborhood."

· 856 ·

Choose a business partner the way you choose
a tennis partner. Select someone who's
strong where you are weak.

· 857 ·

Call a nursing home or retirement center
and ask for a list of the residents who
seldom get mail or visitors. Send them
a card several times a year.
Sign it, "Someone who thinks
you are very special."

· 858 ·

Make duplicates of all important keys.

· 859 ·

Read a lot when you're on vacation,
but nothing that has to do with your business.

· 860 ·

Put the knife in the jelly *before* putting it
in the peanut butter when you
make a sandwich.

· 861 ·

Don't buy a house in a neighborhood
where you have to pay first
before pumping gas.

· 862 ·

Remember that what's right isn't always
popular, and what's popular
isn't always right.

· 863 ·

Before buying a house or renting an apartment,
check the water pressure by turning on
the faucets and the shower and
then flushing the toilet.

· 864 ·

Overestimate travel time by 15 percent.

· 865 ·

Properly fitting shoes should feel good
as soon as you try them on. Don't believe the
salesperson who says, "They'll be fine as
soon as you break them in."

· 866 ·

Schedule your bachelor party at least
two days before your wedding.

· 867 ·

Get a haircut a week before
the big interview.

· 868 ·

Spend your life lifting people up,
not putting people down.

· 869 ·

Never interrupt when you
are being flattered.

· 870 ·

Remember that
great love and
great achievements
involve great risk.

· 871 ·

Don't pick up after your children.
That's their job.

· 872 ·

Own a cowboy hat.

· 873 ·

Own a comfortable chair for reading.

· 874 ·

Own a set of good kitchen knives.

· 875 ·

In business or in life,
don't follow the wagon tracks too closely.

· 876 ·

Get your name off mailing lists by
writing to: Mail Preference Service,
P.O. Box 9008,
New York, NY 11735-9099.

· 877 ·

Brush your teeth before
putting on your tie.

· 878 ·

Never risk what you can't afford to lose.

· 879 ·

Never buy anything electrical
at a flea market.

· 880 ·

Don't trust a woman who doesn't close
her eyes when you kiss her.

· 881 ·

Never tell a man he's losing his hair.
He already knows.

· 882 ·

Learn to use a needle and thread, a steam iron,
and an espresso machine.

· 883 ·

Remember that the "suggested
retail price" seldom is.

· 884 ·

Never say,
"My child would never do that."

· 885 ·

Once a year, go someplace you've
never been before.

· 886 ·

Replace the batteries in smoke alarms
every January First.

· 887 ·

Never order chicken-fried steak in a place
that doesn't have a jukebox.

· 888 ·

Remember that ignorance is expensive.

· 889 ·

Keep candles and matches in the kitchen and
bedroom in case of power failure.

· 890 ·

If you make a lot of money, put it to use
helping others while you are living. That is
wealth's greatest satisfaction.

· 891 ·

Listen to your critics. They will keep you
focused and innovative.

· 892 ·

Never tell a person who's experiencing
deep sorrow, "I know how you feel."
You don't.

· 893 ·

Remember that not getting what you want is
sometimes a stroke of good luck.

· 894 ·

Never say anything to a news reporter that
you don't want to see on the front page
of your local paper. Comments made
"off the record" seldom are.

· 895 ·

Remember the old proverb,
"Out of debt, out of danger."

· 896 ·

Don't allow your dog to bark and
disturb the neighbors.

· 897 ·

When declaring your rights, don't
forget your responsibilities.

· 898 ·

Remember that what you give will afford you
more pleasure than what you get.

· 899 ·

Display your street number prominently
on your mailbox or house in case
emergency vehicles need to find you.

· 900 ·

Think twice before accepting a job
that requires you to work in an
office with no windows.

· 901 ·

Remember that everyone you meet wears
an invisible sign. It reads, "Notice me.
Make me feel important."

· 902 ·

Never hire someone you wouldn't
invite home to dinner.

· 903 ·

Perform your job better than anyone else can.
That's the best job security I know.

· 904 ·

When camping or hiking, never leave
evidence that you were there.

· 905 ·

Dress respectfully
when attending church.

· 906 ·

Never ask an accountant, lawyer, or
doctor professional questions
in a social setting.

· 907 ·

When someone has provided you with
exceptional service, write a note
to his or her boss.

· 908 ·

When you've learned that a good friend
is ill, don't ask him about it.
Let him tell you first.

· 909 ·

For easier reading in motel rooms,
pack your own 100-watt light bulb.

· 910 ·

If you lend someone money, make sure the
person's character exceeds the collateral.

· 911 ·

Whether it's life or a horse that throws you,
get right back on.

· 912 ·

Be cautious telling people how contented
and happy you are. Many will resent it.

· 913 ·

Hang up if someone puts you on hold
to take a "call waiting."

· 914 ·

Accept the fact that regardless of
how many times you are right,
you will sometimes be wrong.

· 915 ·

Every once in a while ask yourself
the question, If money weren't a
consideration, what would
I like to be doing?

· 916 ·

Learn the rules.
Then break some.

· 917 ·

No matter how old you get, hug and kiss your
mother whenever you greet her.

· 918 ·

Watch "The Andy Griffith Show" to help
keep things in perspective.

· 919 ·

Put love notes in your child's lunch box.

· 920 ·

Encourage anyone who is trying to
improve mentally, physically,
or spiritually.

· 921 ·

Remember that half the joy of
achievement is in the anticipation.

· 922 ·

Go to rodeos.

· 923 ·

Go to donkey basketball games.

· 924 ·

Go to chili cook-offs.

· 925 ·

Order an L. L. Bean catalog. Write to
L. L. Bean, Freeport, ME 04033.

· 926 ·

Remember that the best relationship is
one where your love for each other is
greater than your need for each other.

· 927 ·

When you need assistance, ask this way:
"I've got a problem. I wonder if you would be
kind enough to help me?"

· 928 ·

Get involved with your local government.
As someone said, "Politics is too important to
be left to the politicians."

· 929 ·

Order a Sundance catalog. Write to
Customer Service Center, 1909 South
4250 West, Salt Lake City, UT 84104.

· 930 ·

Never swap your integrity for
money, power, or fame.

· 931 ·

Never tell an off-color joke
when ladies are present.

· 932 ·

Never sell yourself short.

· 933 ·

Fool someone on April First.

· 934 ·

Never remind someone of a kindness or act
of generosity you have shown him or her.
Bestow a favor and then forget it.

· 935 ·

Help your children set up their own savings
and checking accounts by age 16.

· 936 ·

Learn to play "Amazing Grace"
on the piano.

· 937 ·

Put on old clothes before you
get out the paint brushes.

· 938 ·

Never be ashamed of your patriotism.

· 939 ·

Never be ashamed of honest tears.

· 940 ·

Never be ashamed of laughter that's too
loud or singing that's too joyful.

· 941 ·

Always try the house dressing.

· 942 ·

Don't trust your memory;
write it down.

· 943 ·

When you get really angry,
stick your hands in your pockets.

· 944 ·

Do all you can to increase the
salaries of good teachers.

· 945 ·

At least once, date a woman
with beautiful red hair.

· 946 ·

Visit friends and relatives when they are
in the hospital. You only need
to stay a few minutes.

· 947 ·

Watch the movie
Mr. Smith Goes to Washington.

· 948 ·

Watch the movie *Regarding Henry.*

· 949 ·

Never leave a youngster in the car
without taking the car keys.

· 950 ·

Don't think that sending a gift or flowers
substitutes for your presence.

· 951 ·

When visiting a small town at lunch time,
choose the café on the square.

· 952 ·

Attach a small Christmas wreath
to your car's grill
on the first day of December.

· 953 ·

Never ask a barber if you need a haircut.

· 954 ·

Truth is serious business.
When criticizing others, remember that
a little goes a long way.

· 955 ·

Never buy a piece of jewelry that costs
more than $100 without doing
a little haggling.

· 956 ·

When your children are learning
to play musical instruments,
buy them good ones.

· 957 ·

Judge your success by
what you had to give up
in order to get it.

· 958 ·

Never "borrow" so much as a pencil
from your workplace.

· 959 ·

Become a tourist for a day in your own hometown.
Take a tour. See the sights.

· 960 ·

Don't confuse foolishness with bravery.

· 961 ·

Don't mistake kindness for weakness.

· 962 ·

Answer the easy questions first.

· 963 ·

Don't discuss domestic problems at work.

· 964 ·

A racehorse that consistently runs just a second
faster than another horse is worth millions of
dollars more. Be willing to give that extra
effort that separates the winner from
the one in second place.

· 965 ·

Create a smoke-free office and home.

· 966 ·

Let some things remain mysterious.

· 967 ·

Never ignore evil.

· 968 ·

Be especially courteous and patient
with older people.

· 969 ·

Remember this statement by Coach Lou Holtz,
"Life is 10 percent what happens to me and
90 percent how I react to it."

· 970 ·

Travel. See new places, but remember to
take along an open mind.

· 971 ·

Never get a tattoo.

· 972 ·

Never eat a sugared doughnut
when wearing a dark suit.

· 973 ·

Call before dropping in on
friends and family.

· 974 ·

When you are away from home and hear
church bells, think of someone
who loves you.

· 975 ·

When friends offer to help, let them.

· 976 ·

Never decide to do nothing
just because you can only do a little.
Do what you can.

· 977 ·

Acknowledge a gift, no matter how small.

· 978 ·

Every now and then,
bite off more than you can chew.

· 979 ·

Remember that your character
is your destiny.

· 980 ·

Approach love and cooking with reckless abandon.

· 981 ·

Grind it out. Hanging on just one second
longer than your competition
makes you the winner.

· 982 ·

Buy and use your customers' products.

· 983 ·

Be better prepared than you think
you need to be.

· 984 ·

Buy a small, inexpensive camera.
Take it with you everywhere.

· 985 ·

Let your handshake be as binding
as a signed contract.

· 986 ·

Keep and file
the best business letters you receive.

· 987 ·

Pay the extra money for the best seats
at a play or concert.

· 988 ·

Give handout materials after your
presentation, never before.

· 989 ·

Never buy anything from a rude
salesperson, no matter how
much you want it.

· 990 ·

Get a flu shot.

· 991 ·

Worry makes for a hard pillow.
When something's troubling you,
before going to sleep, jot down three
things you can do the next day
to help solve the problem.

· 992 ·

Buy a red umbrella. It's easier to
find among all the black ones,
and it adds a little color to rainy days.

· 993 ·

Hire people more for their judgment
than for their talents.

· 994 ·

Love someone who doesn't deserve it.

· 995 ·

Every so often, go where you can hear a
wooden screen door slam shut.

· 996 ·

When you mean no, say it in a way
that's not ambiguous.

· 997 ·

Attend a high school football game.
Sit near the band.

· 998 ·

Give children toys that are powered by
their imagination, not by batteries.

· 999 ·

Remember that your child's character is like
good soup. Both are homemade.

· 1000 ·

Never open a restaurant.

· 1001 ·

When you're buying something that
you only need to buy once,
buy the best you can afford.

· 1002 ·

As soon as you get married, start saving
for your children's education.

· 1003 ·

Reject and condemn prejudice based on
race, gender, religion, or age.

· 1004 ·

Choose a seat in the row next to the
emergency exit when flying.
You will get more leg room.

· 1005 ·

Get involved with Habitat for Humanity
and help build housing for the poor.
Call 1-800-HABITAT.

· 1006 ·

You may dress unconventionally, but remember,
the more strangely you dress,
the better you have to be.

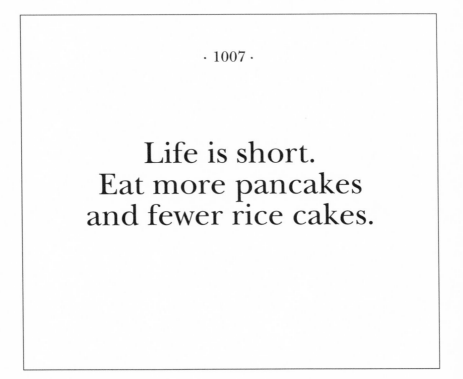

· 1007 ·

Life is short.
Eat more pancakes
and fewer rice cakes.

· 1008 ·

Be suspicious of a boss who schedules meetings
instead of making decisions.

· 1009 ·

Carry three business cards in your wallet.

· 1010 ·

Regardless of the situation,
react with class.

· 1011 ·

For emergencies, always have a quarter
in your pocket and a ten-dollar bill
hidden in your wallet.

· 1012 ·

Don't overfeed horses or brothers-in-law.

· 1013 ·

Be able to hit consistently four out of
five at the free-throw line.

· 1014 ·

Become the kind of person who brightens
a room just by entering it.

· 1015 ·

Remember the observation of William James
that the deepest principle in human nature
is the craving to be appreciated.

· 1016 ·

Buy raffle tickets, candy bars, and baked goods
from students who are raising money
for school projects.

· 1017 ·

Be wary of the man who's
"all hat and no cattle."

· 1018 ·

Borrow a box of puppies for an afternoon and
take them to visit the residents of a
retirement home. Stand back
and watch the smiles.

· 1019 ·

Reread Thoreau's *Walden*.

· 1020 ·

When there's a piano to be moved,
don't reach for the stool.

· 1021 ·

Someone will always be looking at you as
an example of how to behave.
Don't let that person down.

· 1022 ·

Go on blind dates.
Remember, that's how I met your mother.

· 1023 ·

Root for the home team.

· 1024 ·

Follow your own star.

· 1025 ·

Remember the ones who love you.

· 1026 ·

Go home for the holidays.

· 1027 ·

Don't get too big for your britches.

· 1028 ·

Call your dad.

Dear Reader,

If you received advice from your parents or grandparents that was especially meaningful and you would like to share it with other readers, please write and tell me about it.

I look forward to hearing from you.

H. Jackson Brown, Jr.
P. O. Box 150155
Nashville, TN 37215